So Much of Everything

Jenn Koiter

Early response to *So Much of Everything*

"With fearless candor lit by insight, Jenn Koiter catches herself off guard, revealing how our culture works us up, how what's real out there drops us: "the game gives shape to your desire, though your desire means nothing to the game." An engrossing experience to read, a debut to celebrate!"
  - Eleanor Wilner, author of *Before Our Eyes: New and Selected Poems, 1975–2017*

"*She inhabits the superlative,* Jenn Koiter writes in this astute and lucent book whose chief concern is exactly that: *muchness*. The over-the-top costumings and accoutrements of a 6' 4" pin-up girl. The insanely sensate experience that is a walk down a Dehli street. The amplitudes by which memory is measured. The fullness of life. The abundance of loss. These poems don't flinch from anyone's punch, not even their own. If you don't know where to begin, start with "The Survivor"; it's the most stunning elegy I've read in a decade. At its most profound, *So Much of Everything* is a hymn to the aggregate complexity of mortality: it may be so much but it is never—*not ever*— enough."
  - Jill Alexander Essbaum, author of *Hausfrau*

"*What will I do with darkness in this new life?* is the question that ends Jenn Koiter's first poem in her aptly titled book SO MUCH OF EVERYTHING. That question frames all that follows in this funny and harrowing book that is, in the end, a hymn to life. 'The Survivor' is the title of the long, magnificent sequence near the book's end, and this book is, indeed, a learner's guide to survival."
  -Jim Moore, author of *Prognosis*

"In this utterly gorgeous debut collection, Jenn Koiter has arrived as a poet whose voice is only matched by her remarkable intelligence, and whose heart carries the day. I especially love the "Messy Girl" series and the elegies to poets Jake Adam York and Craig Arnold; and I find that the genius of this book is its capacity to hold messiness in general—to hold all of life, that is to say, in a continuous negative capability. I am in awe of Koiter's technical skill and poetic range; she is a poet of many gifts."
   - David Keplinger, author of *The World to Come*

"Jenn Koiter will take the top of your head off with this dazzling set of poems. She won my heart on first reading because I want to feel every emotion humanly possible when I read poetry. She'll make you laugh; she'll make you cry—all the while stunning you with her originality and wit. I immediately wanted more, so I read it all over again."
   - Grace Cavalieri, *Maryland Poet Laureate*

So Much of Everything © Day Eight, 2021

All poems in the book © Jenn Koiter, 2012-2021

Cover image © Alexandra N Sherman, used by permission of the artist

Book design by Shannon Pallatta

For my parents, for loving me through everything

These poems were written with the timely support of artist residencies at The Kimmel Harding Nelson Center for the Arts and Art342; a Money for Women Grant from the Barbara Deming Memorial Fund; and a Jacob K. Javits Fellowship from the U.S. Department of Education.

I am overwhelmed with gratitude, especially to Jane Hilberry and Steve Schroeder for helping untangle my manuscript; to Robert Bettman, for his commitment to creating a beautiful book; to the members of WWLD, my formative workshop; to my many teachers over the years, particularly Eleanor Wilner and Jenny Factor, who kept me going; to Craig Arnold and Jake York, for taking me by the hand for a time; and to my mentors, family, and friends for helping this work along and for celebrating with me—achievement without community is hollow.

Thank you to the publications that first published poems in this book:

"Outliers" in *Anon*
"A Litany in Time of Divorce" in *Anti-*
"I push my foot into my boot, and you die" in *Anti-Heroin Chic*
"How are you holding up?" in *Anti-Heroin Chic*
"I speed, late as usual" in *Autumn Sky Poetry Daily*
"The Makeover" in *Barrelhouse*
"The Shift" in *Bateau*
"My instructor says dead body pose" in *Bourgeon*
"Easter Night" in *Bourgeon*
"After Thanksgiving" in *Bourgeon*
"Samsara" in *Bourgeon*
"Rapture Scare" in *Copper Nickel*
"Forget Rome" and "Farmer's Market Elegy" in *Eunoia*

"Nightmares Plague The Messy Girl as She Travels" in *Gastropoda*

"The last time I saw you…" in *Gastropoda*

"Why I Switched the Music Off" in *Mausoleum*

"Candy Jones Begins" in *No Tell Motel*

"Candy Jones Confronts the Passage of Time" in *No Tell Motel*

"Candy Jones Knows How to Calm Down" in *No Tell Motel*

"Ghazal, with Accessories" in *No Tell Motel*

"True/False" in *No Tell Motel*

"Your absence is no more like hunger" in *One Art*

"Last visit to your house…" in *One Art*

"All I remember about your body" in *One Art*

"A few books, a few candles, a few tools" in *One Art*

"First morning, first week, first thirteen days" in *One Art*

"The Messy Girl Discovers She Is a Gay Camp Icon" in *perhappened*

"Feverish, Candy Jones Sees the Truth of Things" in *Rejection Letters*

"Through Snow" in *Relief*

"Lost Sheep" in *Rock and Sling*

"Reading Tour" in *The Shore*

"The Messy Girl Drives Eastward, With Impending Migraine"
    in *South Dakota Review*

"Prayer With Mathematics" in *South Dakota Review*

"Early Dinner Ending With a Line from Thomas Merton"
    in *South Dakota Review*

"Candy Jones's Second Personality Has Opinions About Candy Jones"
    in *Sledgehammer*

"Scream" in *Stone of Madness*

"Because you were alive the last time I saw you"
    in *Twin Pies Literary*

Jenn Koiter is the 2021 winner of the DC Poet Project, an open-to-all poetry competition created by the non-profit Day Eight. The competition occurs connected to a poetry reading series organized by Day Eight in partnership with the DC Public Library, Anacostia Coordinating Council, and Brink Media. In 2021, Day Eight was funded to conduct the project by grant from the DC Commission on the Arts and Humanities.

Between January and May 2021, five reading series events were held featuring poets John Johnson, Reil, Naomi Ayala, E. Ethelbert Miller, Holly Karapetkova (Arlington poet laureate), Kim B. Miller (Prince William County poet laureate), Grace Cavalieri (Maryland poet laureate), Lori Tsang, Jane Schapiro, Luther Jett, Marlena Chertock and Malik Thompson. Each reading series event included a connected open mic, and at the end of each event the featuring poets selected one open mic reader to appear at the culminating reading. Due to the coronavirus, as the earlier readings in the series the culminating reading was held online, Saturday, May 22nd. More than a 120 attended and voted Jenn Koiter winner of the 2021 DC Poet Project.

So Much of Everything takes the reader on a heartbreaking intellectual and emotional journey. I'm reminded of a poem by Venus Thrash, a gorgeous DC-area poet who passed away recently and far too soon. In her poem, Kinstugi, Venus writes, "Every smashed piece can be made whole." Somehow, we make it through.

Thank you to the author, and all of the poets who participated in the 2021 Poet Project, for the opportunity to experience your light.

Robert Bettmann
Director, DC Poet Project
August 2021

SO MUCH OF EVERYTHING

Jenn Koiter

Table of Contents

Easter Night	1
Reading Tour	2
Through Snow	4
The Messy Girl Drives Eastward, With Impending Migraine	5
Introduction to Dodgeball	6
After Thanksgiving	7
Scream	8
The Messy Girl Carries a Torch For The Boy Who Could Not Stop Washing	9
The Messy Girl Discovers She Is A Gay Camp Icon	11
The Makeover	12
After the Makeover	14
The Messy Girl's Hair Is A Mess	15
Live Portrait	16
Candy Jones Lays It All Out	20
Ghazal, with Accessories	22
Candy Jones Reminds The Ladies What To Keep In Mind	23
Pantoum, With Outfits	27
Sonnet Confronting the Passage of Time	29
Feverish, Candy Jones Sees the Truth of Things	30

Candy Jones Knows How to Calm Down	31
It's All Starting to Come Back to Candy Jones	32
Arlene Grant Has Opinions About Candy Jones	34
True/False	36
The Messy Girl Feels at Home in Delhi	39
Samsara	42
Rapture Scare	43
Outliers	44
Lost Sheep	45
Looking for Prester John	46
Early Dinner Ending with a Line from Thomas Merton	48
Rouault in L.A.	50
Forget Rome	52
A Litany in Time of Divorce	54
Why I Switched the Music Off	55
Nightmares Plague The Messy Girl As She Travels	56
The Messy Girl Forgets Her Dreams	57
The Survivor	59
The Shift	77
Prayer With Mathematics	78
Farmer's Market Elegy	80

EASTER NIGHT

After a long sleep, I wake,
long after the chill of sunrise services in parks,
after high heels sinking into wet grass,
after even late morning services,
hum and shuffle of warm pews.

I have slept through frilly little-girl dresses
and grown up hats, through hugs and handshakes
of smiling strangers, through earnest, quavery hymns,
through *He is risen* and *risen, indeed,*
through the slow egress of crowded parking lots.

There exists a tribe of monkeys
that gathers before sunrise, looking east,
and when the sun crests the horizon,
they all clap.

I wish I were a woman who could
worship the sun rising.
I would stand with them and cheer.

Though someone must greet the dark
each day, and how much more
today, when all is new?

Since yesterday, the earth has tilted.
The day's last light curves
differently over my arm
on its habitual armrest, then dims
and dims to night.

What will I do with darkness in this new life?

READING TOUR
for Craig and Jake

Two poets go on a road trip. This is not a joke,
though there is laughter. It is a good road trip,
maybe the best road trip, were it possible
to measure such things.

Both poets are tall and beautiful,
which always helps. They are both smart.
They know things. And because
they inhabit the same strange sub-subculture
that is American poetry in the early aughts,
they have enough in common
to make conversation easy, yet
enough difference to keep things interesting.
They stop somewhere and read poems, then drive
and stop and read poems. It is heaven.
Also they have dried figs, five pounds of them,
and they eat them for three days straight.

One of the poets will lose himself so well
we cannot find him. (This is not a metaphor.)
The other's body will betray him
suddenly, irredeemably.
They will both be unlucky, at the end.

But on this road trip, they are the luckiest.
They have found each other, and in each other, taste
friendship's bright tang and slow ferment.
They will each tell the story of it for years.

It's not really a story. Just two friends becoming better friends, which is a not-story worth telling over and over, even, perhaps especially, now, when there is no one left on earth who remembers the taste of those figs.

THROUGH SNOW

I can see only so far,
despite the headlights, despite the wipers
brushing snow aside with a soft thud.
The air is thick with it, like a mind thick with sleep
when the phone rang at three a.m., a friend calling
to tell me the car crashed, her mother died, her voice
thick with grief. I thought she was someone else at first,
but I also heard the voice of an old friend
who no longer calls me back
when a student called and said only my name.
I guess at where a parking space might be.
Snow covers everything. Across the alley,
at the back door, the key sticks
in the cold lock. I freeze. I don't know
whether this is really where I live.

THE MESSY GIRL DRIVES EASTWARD, WITH IMPENDING MIGRAINE

Lines of birds shift in the air like words that cannot stay still
on the page, latecomers looking for a place
in an already crowded field. What else is wrong?
She might be coming down with a cold. (There was a man
    with a cold.)
She might be pregnant. (There was a broken condom.)
Nausea flickers. Her leg and arm prickle and numb.
When she tiptoed out this morning, it was under a bright
    blue western sky,
but all through Nebraska, the mist is unrelenting.
There is no sunset, no dusk, only darker
and darker gray. Clusters of headlights thin to pass her
two by two, already too bright for her eyes,
perhaps because her eyes yield
their own light, throwing halos around
everything but her.

INTRODUCTION TO DODGEBALL

The game wants to be played. The way a story presses you to tell it. Without you, it is the mancala board's dusty hollows, is pitz or faro, is dice in Egyptian tombs. You play because you want to, because, from the opening rush to the last woman out, your body knows exactly what to do. The court simplifies. Catch. Drill. Hold the corner, scamper, hunker down. Whether you forget yourself in a flurry of purple no-sting dodgeballs, or move with conscious delight at being in a body, being in your body, is entirely up to you. If you sit down, the balls will come. If you want to be the best, learn how best to submit, how best to be complicit with the game as it moves you. Pour your everything into this. The game gives shape to your desire, though your desire means nothing to the game, dispassionate arbiter of fenced courts, of rec centers reserved from three to seven, of gymnasia poorly ventilated. It will discard you without a second thought, leaving you to watch from the court's edge. O watch well. O touch each one gently when she has to stop and watch the game go on without her.

AFTER THANKSGIVING

I am eating
leftover brandied cranberries
mixed into plain yogurt
not because I
particularly like them
but because
my mother does
& I feel closer to her
when I eat them
than I do when we talk
sometimes & because
my mother will die
someday & I will need
all the practice
I can manage to draw
close to her when
she isn't there

SCREAM

I hear stories of my early childhood as if they happened to someone else. How, when Jennifer didn't want to go to daycare, she lay on the asphalt by her father's truck, screaming her three-year-old lungs out. How her father learned to sit patiently behind the wheel, passenger door open, and wait till she grew calm and climbed in. How Jennifer marched into daycare each morning and shrugged her coat to the floor. How another child always hung it up. How Jennifer told the other children when it was time to play with this toy or that. How, on what would be the last day of daycare, Jennifer discovered she could climb out of the window on the second floor and slide down the drainpipe on the side of the building. How parents arrived to find their children in an orderly line, climbing and sliding, Jennifer running a tight ship while the teacher slept it off in the coat closet.

What I do remember is a dream. A tarantula crawled up my arm to my shoulder, the teacher beside me, her big blond head. She pulled the spider's body away, but some of the legs stuck to my shoulder. *Ah, ah,* I said, the legs quivered and clung, and I could not scream.

THE MESSY GIRL CARRIES A TORCH FOR THE BOY WHO COULD NOT STOP WASHING

She reads about him in a medical journal,
where she often finds her people,
and falls for him immediately.
She writes to him
and waits. Waiting stretches her
thin, thinner, heart pounding
and never hungry, alone
in her room for days.

She knows he's busy, what with all the washing.
She's certain he will understand her obsession,
dull, most of the time, like any madness.
She's certain he will understand
her preference for the reflection of the moon
over the moon.

She's running. She's never been in better shape.
He's busy, but surely she'll be able to keep up
once she can run a mile,
two miles, five.
She might as well use her time for something.
She's been dreaming about his childhood again.
By the bed, on torn-open envelopes, notes
she doesn't remember making:
Unconvinced he touched each sidewalk crack,
the child trudges two whole miles back.
She knows too much about his childhood.

There are days she wonders
what it would be like to want
because she wants to. There are days
she worries scab after scab.
There are days fear wicks across her mind
like red wine on white linen.
She moves through a persistent whir
and she ignores it,
sick with
and sick of
the fever that won't burn off,
the fugue in two voices:
chase and
flee.

She's flipping through medical journals again.
She contemplates a fling
with HM, who won't remember anyway.
She meets Anna O. for coffee.
What wouldn't she give to breathe
like the Buddha? She debates free will
with the three Christs of Ypsilanti instead.

Still, there are days. She knows too much.
She's running. She's certain.
What wouldn't she give.

THE MESSY GIRL DISCOVERS SHE IS A GAY CAMP ICON

It all makes sense now: the so many nights
that end in weeping, one false eyelash
half-unglued, mascara running, then
caught with an old used Kleenex,
the booze, the pills, the persistent rumor
she's had two ribs removed,
her image in that Warhol polaroid
exhibited in Krakow, ghost white with a deep red lip.
She googles herself and reads the headlines:
Messy Girl Musical In The Works! and
The Messy Girl Is Done Marrying Gay Men.
Finally, she can throw that violent tantrum
at Heathrow Airport, collapse on set
from nervous exhaustion, take to her bed the whole week
every month, cramping and farting and calling for dinner
in bed, the sheets crusty with old food
and menstrual blood. Though first she must get ready
for the show. She puts on
addiction like a rhinestone bustier, suffering
like a sheer black backless bodysuit.
And her love affairs are an earring, an earring,
and high high heels. What can the fanboys do but cheer,
what can she do but strut onstage:
too much hair, too much skin, too much woman
for anyone to handle?

THE MAKEOVER
A found poem from The Swan, *season one*

I.
You've seen how far these women have come,
but how far will they go?
The key to getting Rachel to the pageant is
to bring out her femininity.
She thinks she's average.
She is a little average,
but when she's happy, she's a very beautiful person.
Beth's new smile is the first step
in feminizing her face.
Andrea's emotional outburst has put her
transformation in jeopardy.
Marnie has a tired look.
It's going to take a lot of work
to get Marnie pageant-ready.
Beth's relationship with
her husband is the next hurdle
in her transformation.
Kristy does not feel partnered
by her husband. Will revenge be enough
to motivate her?
Kelly needs a lot of work today.
She doesn't have the greatest genetics.
In her own words, she looks like a witch.
Kathy is actually a very beautiful woman, underneath
all the (dare I say) less beautiful features.
Dawn really needs more feminization.
It's going to take a lot of work.
Marnie hasn't left her room in three days.
And Andrea does not stick to the program.

II.
You have been judged
on beauty, poise, and overall transformation.
What is going through that
very pretty head of yours, Kristy?
Do you really feel
like the outside finally matches the inside?
You think you'll be belly dancing now?
The time has come, Cindy.
Behind that curtain, there is a mirror.
Andrea, please step up to the curtain.
I'm not coming with you,
not this time. Go,
walk to the curtain, Kelly.
Step up to the curtain, Merline.

AFTER THE MAKEOVER

Kelly, I have one question for you: What have you done with Kelly?
 -Amanda Bynam, host of The Swan

You surely didn't think she'd let you walk
the catwalk without her, the woman in gray,
ill-fitting underwear whose image hovered
beside you on the stage, letting all her flab hang out
while you vogued in your blue bikini? the one
the emcee congratulated you over and over
for overcoming, her imperfect, unsmiling face
behind you on the back wall?
You thought she was gone, but now
she's followed you home, erected
a crude shack in the backyard – not much,
but it keeps the rain out –found a dumpster
behind a bakery, filled each night with unsold baguettes.
(You'd be amazed what some people throw out.)
Your son tells her everything – the name of the girl
he has a crush on, the story he wrote
when he should have been studying math – then
kisses her on the cheek. And at night, when you turn
to the still-warm other half of the bed, your husband
has just snuck out the back. But it's you
she most wants to talk to. Each day, she digs
through the bakery dumpster till she finds
your favorite raisin bread. In case
you finally steal out to see her.
In case you want to cheat, and have some carbs.

THE MESSY GIRL'S HAIR IS A MESS

If only they would stay
lacquered in her retro beehive, but no,
the hairs are everywhere. They nest in the threads
of the toothpaste tube, tangle in the lint trap,
form a dyed-red trail onto the bedroom carpet
for other hairs to follow.
One fallen hair tickles her bare arm,
as if she's just walked through a spider's web.
She's found hairs in her food so often
at that Indian dive across the tracks
that when it isn't there, she adds
one of her own to make it right.
The TV hairs are perfect.
Falling strands glisten
like they were just secreted
by a silkworm, have yet to harden into silk.
But that's not really how it works.
The Messy Girl has seen pictures: a silkworm
suspended in a loose mat
like hair pulled from a bristle brush,
weaving its sticky salivary tomb.
She tries to wash her hands
of this whole mess, but a slick of wet hair
rushes from the faucet, swirls in the sink
and down the drain, sleek and strong
and sickening.

LIVE PORTRAIT

I.
The artist says he will see
only you, and you
should look only at him.
His gaze is strong, it could
carry, even throw you
high enough for a triple axel,
perfect landing.
You have waited so
long for this, to be watched
like this, and his gaze is heavy
as disappointment, heavy as lust
and the long wait.

II.
You are not relaxed
and do not need to relax.
Drive your discomfort
into your hands.

III.
Mostly, of course, he
looks at the portrait.
Everyone looks
at the portrait, from
the delicate first lines
to the violent end
when he crawls over
his own work,
charcoal crushed
under his palm,

his eyes flicking
up at you. This is best.
The portrait can bear
the weight of all that
looking, the portrait
first an eye, then an idea
of you, smudged
clear to the paper's edge,
the portrait (let's face it) more
important than the artist
or you, especially you.

IV.
No one gets to pick
what someone else observes.

V.
The artist's hands will never be clean.
The same gesture, always, whatever
he is making: crushing
the charcoal, breathing
the brown cloud, the same
charcoal that recreates, on this paper,
the model is under his fingernails,
is between his teeth.
The artist will never be clean.
He belongs to the city. O the mess!
O the bodies! O the city grit!

VI.
Will you remember this? he asks
Will you remember
it was raining?

Say *Yes*

(but it is not raining)

VII.
Dolphins belong
underwater and
cannot breathe
underwater.
Of course you belong
here. Breathe
a deep breath. Deep
breath. Hold.

THE CANDY JONES POEMS

Note: With the exception of "True/False," this section consists of found poems created using sentences from books by Candy Jones, 1940s cover girl, mid century beauty expert, and subject of a CIA mind control conspiracy theory in the 1970s.

CANDY JONES LAYS IT ALL OUT

Let's learn the rules of the game.
    First of all, let me request you sharpen your scissors
  and remove all belt loops. Buttons
are low cost tattletales. Be wary
of wearing any accessories
    that you can't handle. For emergencies,
  a tiny sewing kit should be on hand.
    Make a critical rundown of your imperfect features.
Hold your stomach absolutely flat
    and tuck your buttocks in neatly.
Pay attention to your shoulders. Pay attention
     to the condition of your shoes.
  Observe swimsuit ads
  and learn to stand gracefully
with your knees together.
    Practice sitting
     and standing in front of a full-length mirror
  until you are certain
   that you place your legs in their most becoming positions.
And please don't wear a fur piece.
    Take a good look
at your hemline.
  Skirts should be worn
  modestly short.
    No Kitty Foyle costumes permitted!
Make certain to remember that nothing is forever
   except that you are a woman.
Do look crisp and tidy,
  but not unfeminine. You are female
    and by nature and the natural law
you are meant to be feminine.

  Take and make the time to beautify
 all parts of your body.
But go a little easy on the eye-goo.
   Makeup should be applied to dramatize
 the eyes and lips, but not
to give the effect of a lady spy.

Don't laugh…
  there are such things.

GHAZAL, WITH ACCESSORIES

Make your first appearance upon your arrival wearing a hat.
Even if hats are not your favorite accessory, wear a hat.

Your accessories should be kept to a truthful minimum.
A good rule of thumb is: don't wear jewelry with a hat.

Don't clutter up the area around your face
with too much detail. (Egad, Mabel! That hat!)

I feel the same way about wearing flowers in one's hair.
Yesterday's orchid – not unlike yesterday's newspaper – is old hat.

Your goal is pureness of line and complete simplicity.
Choose your jewelry accents sparingly. Don't wear a hat.

CANDY JONES REMINDS THE LADIES WHAT TO KEEP IN MIND

Don't start with a rush or a solemn vow
That you'll soon be teaching the others "how."

   Sagging bosom
   Drooping buttocks
   Heavy thighs
   Double chin
   Bulging hips
   Protruding abdomen
                                              Kate hates tight tapes.

REDHEADS BRUNETTES BROWNETTES BLONDES

                     Dick tipped the tippet and dripped it.

NAVY white, navy, yellow, white, mustard, sand, red/white, maize, black chartreuse white, apple navy/white, green black, beige BEIGE topaz, black, hot pink, rust, vivid luggage tan, mint green orange, black, blue, black, off-white, coral, brown turquoise GRAY

The clothes moth's mouth closed.

A lamp without a shade;
 a cake without icing;
    champagne without bubbles;
      television without sound;
         a romance without kisses;
            a prom without a corsage.

This is the day your dreams come true… wedding bells… rice… and the words "I do."

Sneezing　　　　　　　Itching　　　　　　　Wheezing
　　　Swollen eyelids　　　　　Coughing
　Breakouts of skin　　Dry, chapped lips　　Scalp rash.

It's because –
Just because.
Because.
Because-because-because.
　　　　　　　　　Such slipshod speech as she speaks.

A bear, a beaut, a blinder, a brick, a catchy number, a corker, a daisy, a danderoo, a duckeroo, a fetcher, a knockout, a lookerino, a lulu, a peachagulu [a what?] a striker and… and so on.

　　　　　　　　　　WRONG. WRONG. WRONG.

Too fast Too slow Too loud Too weak　　Hesitation

Lack of variety or monotony of tone

Lack of variety, monotony

Hoarse　　　　　Breathy　　　　　Flat　　　　　Nasal

Throaty and guttural　　　Unsatisfactory
Strained and harsh　　　　Unsatisfactory
Careless or slovenly　　　 Unsatisfactory
Thin and weak　　　　　　Unsatisfactory
Dull and lifeless　　　　　 Unsatisfactory

Geese cackle, cattle low, crows caw, cocks crow. The needy needle woman needn't wheedle.

Oh, how they envy her, one and all
That popular girl, the belle of the ball.

                                        Excuses, excuses.
  Stop, stop, stop!

bony-fleshy-rounded-firm-slender-indented-curveless-fleshy-firm-flabby-protruding-flat-firm-flabby-fleshy-sway-back-straight-spindly-flat-narrow-firm-rounded-lumpy-fleshy-flabby-firm-flabby-fleshy-sagging-flat-rounded-lumpy-full-heavy-fleshy-flabby-ridged-firm-slim-rounded-fleshy-firm-slim-knocked-bowed-knobby-large-firm-rounded-straight-muscular-fleshy- small-slim-full-heavy-fleshy-firm-bony-small-medium-large-bony-flat-trim-wide-fleshy-

Some shun sunshine, some shun sleep.

                              HERE'S WHAT I HAVE
                              HERE'S WHAT I NEED
                              HERE'S WHAT I HAVE
                              HERE'S WHAT I NEED

candy	chocolate
doughnuts	fried foods
gravy	mayonnaise
nuts	pastries
soda pop	whipped cream

Skoh!   Shah!   Gash!   Gawg!

The sea ceaseth, but it sufficeth us.

>   wistful, sad, aloof, pouty, elegant,
>   annoyed, sick,
>   coy, cunning, dreamy,
>   blase, amused,
>   gay or
>   blank.

The shock of the rigged quiz shows.
Payola and its involvement of many of her teen-age heroes.
The mushrooming spread of broken marriages.
The growing display of pornography.
The statistics of juvenile crime and delinquency.
The blight of mental illness in young people.
The divorce rate.
Teen-age mothers of illegitimate babies.
The high percentage of young men rejected by the Armed Services.
And on and on.

So, if this girl sounds a bit like you,
Take our advice on what to do!

>   ... a ... e ... i ... o ... u.

PANTOUM, WITH OUTFITS

In the moonlight, any woman can look a little like Deborah Kerr.
Your jewelry will be precious and superb. Gloves complete
    the costume look.
You want to look dreamy, soft and feminine. Today, studied
    simplicity is the key.
A beret pulled low on the forehead is an excellent choice.

Gloves complete the costume look. Your jewelry will be
    precious and superb.
You owe it to old Joe to look pretty for him.
A beret pulled low on the forehead is an excellent choice.
A turban-draped hat would be an unwise choice.

You owe it to old Joe to look pretty for him.
There isn't anything wrong with low heels – nothing logically
    wrong, that is.
A turban-draped hat would be an unwise choice.
You know immediately when you don't look as nice or as
    sparkling as you should.

There isn't anything wrong with low heels – nothing logically
    wrong, that is.
You are keeping up with her highness, Mrs. Jones, you know.
You know immediately when you don't look as nice or as
    sparkling as you should.
Dresses and blouses pose a problem. The filly must not look frilly.

You are keeping up with her highness, Mrs. Jones, you know.
How would you like to wear a beanbag on your head?
The filly must not look frilly. Dresses and blouses pose a problem.
Shoehorns still serve a purpose. Rouge is used for two purposes.

How would you like to wear a beanbag on your head?
Kid gloves feel like a frozen plastic second skin.
Shoehorns still serve a purpose. Rouge is used for two purposes.
Blood. Perspiration. Lipstick. You have your own hair, plus a wig.

Kid gloves feel like a frozen plastic second skin.
You want to look dreamy, soft and feminine. But, eek, such a dreadful feeling.
Blood. Perspiration. Lipstick.
In the moonlight, any woman can look a little like Deborah Kerr.

SONNET CONFRONTING THE PASSAGE OF TIME

Now we have entered the period of the great reversal.
Hats live in hat boxes, while peasant triangles cover heads
and enter churches. Unpolished shoes, run-down heels,
bare legs by the dozen. Momentarily, I thought it was a
    costume party.
My feet looked like I'd been overseeing a mine.
I am forty-two years old. I'm middle-aged. This to me is revolting.
A mask of a face topping a wreck of a body. I have a golden leg
    stashed away in a closet. And I bet you never knew
… and couldn't have cared less! You're like a bicyclist
picking his way along a road strewn with broken glass.
Don't sparkle too much all over. You're not going to an
    opera, dear.
The lighting will be bright and revealing. Think of a coat as
    a cloak.
Think about the judges. Put yourself in the position of a judge.
Pity the woman with flat feet. One of these years it will
    happen to you.

FEVERISH, CANDY JONES SEES THE TRUTH OF THINGS

They are all fish and give out varying degrees of fishiness. But the plain truth is, they look pretty silly with bosoms. Frequently they lock themselves out of their rooms and even forget their room numbers. They scream and shout, throw things and roll on the floor kicking their heels. They pretend that they are tipsier than they are. They're gay, young, alive-looking. They deny the truth of the bomb. If they seem stubbornly stuck in your head, you can replace them easily by saying a prayer that you may recall from childhood. Sunburn can be fatal to them. My grandmother, who was a doctor, used the power of suggestion to make them disappear. At any rate, they've relented, evidently, in their previous damning of one and all… But make no mistake: they're here to stay. They will dry and stiffen on your skin. They can be had in plaid, or plain for the rain, initialed, jeweled, tooled, shot with metallic or polka dots. They are known as independent contractors by the income-tax people. Defy them, if you can. They have vivid imaginations, which they will exercise on you, slowly at first, to see if you are a willing little fish, ready to bite.

CANDY JONES KNOWS HOW TO CALM DOWN

Steal some
little boy's marbles, toss

a dozen or so
into a frying pan, and let them

fry for a half hour.
Pour them

into a bowl of ice water
and watch them

crack up.
They can be strung

to make a necklace
or bracelet, and all the while

you've fried up
your frustrations and

feel great.

IT'S ALL STARTING TO COME BACK TO CANDY JONES

I.

Dr. Die used his sharp needle. Then this character wandered in, wearing chino pants and sneakers, a seersucker jacket over his arm. Such a manner he had! All five foot five of him. He disappeared for a moment and returned with a stick of white chalk. He placed it over his head and made clicking noises with his tongue. He also kept calling me, "Miss Candy, ma'am." I'll always remember how pale he was and how peaceful his face looked as he lay on the floor in a cold faint next to my bed.

II.

His table manners were impeccable. Really, within forty minutes he had downed four Scotches. He removed his cup from its saucer and placed it on the damask tablecloth. He poured cream into the saucer, added a small amount of sugar and stirred it with his finger. He looked up sharply. He pointed his walking stick at me and with rapid precision snapped his eyelids open and closed-one at a time. First his left, then his right eye stared at me madly. Angrily he stomped his stick on the floor and glared at me. There was only the sound of his movements in the room. Then I felt him feeling my nose. I looked up as he did and saw four peg-shaped points where his front teeth had been.

III.

He's not going to say it. He can't say *anything*. He has or has not dropped dead. Don't kiss him. Or kiss him. Oh, I don't know! Buy a doll, label it with his name and stick pins into it!

Eventually he will ask what's so important about tomorrow. Has he been ill? Was he too shy to phone? Somewhere, he's out there, and the big trick is to find him.

CANDY JONES'S SECOND PERSONALITY HAS OPINIONS ABOUT CANDY JONES

She always looked so well put together and sleek.
A clean, sweet-smelling, impeccably groomed, polite, and
 charming woman.

But that was many years ago.
How was it she had so many clothes?

Really desperate, she had to sell her mink coat.
She got a job.

Hah! So much for single bliss.
I have seldom laughed so hard.

Fanaticism, overdevotion to fashion, can be pretty macabre.
The older she becomes, the more makeup and perfume she wears.

She doesn't appear to be ill
but never seems to be without a pillbox.

Too many women look at but never see themselves
as they really are in their mirrors.

She needs a well-lighted mirror and a standing magnifying
 mirror.
She needs a window by which she can check her outdoors face
 by daylight.

Few things can look so pathetically depressing
as wilted flowers. Yesterday's orchid

– not unlike yesterday's newspaper – is old hat.
　Best she keep it home and press it in her memory book.

TRUE/FALSE

I.
Candy Jones was five-nine. Candy Jones was five-ten. Candy Jones was six feet tall. Six-foot-four. Six-foot-seven in three-inch heels. Candy Jones was famous. Everyone knew Candy Jones, especially servicemen. Candy Jones – tall, tall, famous Candy Jones – could wear a dark wig and not be recognized by anyone. Anyone could be Candy Jones. I could be Candy Jones, and I look nothing like Candy Jones. Candy Jones looks nothing like Candy Jones. I have a friend, a professor friend. Her colleagues treat her with more respect since she started wearing three-inch heels. I never wear three-inch heels. I am five-foot-nine. I am six feet tall when I wear three-inch heels.

II.
Harry Conover invented the Cover Girl. Candy Jones was a Cover Girl. Candy Jones's marketing campaign was genius. Candy-striped dresses and candy-box purses and red and white cards that told Manhattan "Candy Jones Was Here." All that candy-striped shit didn't do a damn thing. Candy Jones was a beauty expert. Candy Jones wrote books. Candy Jones appeared often on the radio. I hate the sound of voices on the radio. Candy Jones joined Long John Nebel's radio show. Then she ran the show alone. I can't not listen. Then she was replaced by Larry King. The voices insist.

III.
When Candy Jones was a child, her mother locked her in a dark closet over and over. Candy Jones was thrilled when her mother came to live with her in Manhattan. Harry Conover was Candy Jones's first husband. He was bisexual. He was gay. Harry Conover would only come on to Candy Jones if he was

drunk. Candy Jones didn't know any better because she never dated much. Candy Jones dated Orson Welles. Orson Welles really just liked playing cards with Candy Jones's darling mother.

IV.

As a child, Candy Jones had imaginary friends. Intelligent children often have imaginary friends. I had no imaginary friends, and my Barbies had complicated sex lives. There was always a good Barbie and a bad Barbie. Neither of their names were Barbie. There was always a good Ken and a bad Ken. Always a bad Ken. The bad Ken is necessary.

V.

One of Candy Jones's imaginary friends was named Arline. Arline was not imaginary. Arline disappeared. Arline stayed. The hypnotist found Arline and brought her back. Arline despised Candy Jones, weak, girly Candy Jones. Arline learned to kill with a hat pin dipped in poison lipstick. Arline learned to kill with her bare hands.

VI.

Candy Jones was never a spy. Candy Jones just carried messages to California. Candy Jones just carried messages to Asia. The messages were vitally important to national security. None of the messages mattered. Candy Jones was captured and tortured by Native Americans. Candy Jones was captured and tortured by Chinese men. No, Chinese women. No, white men in white coats. They sent her to Asia wearing a dark wig. They ran too much electric current through her thumb. They held a lighted candle to her genitals. They programmed her to kill herself in the Bahamas. What mattered was that they could.

VII.

The whole thing was a hoax, concocted by Long John Nebel for their radio show. Candy Jones, who always knew her audience, went along. The whole thing was a hoax, invented by the government to make the Soviets think that they could do everything Candy Jones claimed. Candy Jones made the whole thing up and laughed all the way to her grave. The whole thing was one all-encompassing fuck you. Fuck you, Miss Atlantic City. Fuck you, Model of the Year. Fuck you, lipstick and pancake makeup. Fuck you, girdles and garters and high-heeled shoes. Fuck you, Harry Conover. Fuck you, respectable employment. Fuck you, manners and mores. Fuck you, Mother. Fuck you, Orson Welles.

THE MESSY GIRL FEELS AT HOME IN DELHI

It's not the mess, though
the mess is inescapable, even
in her posh neighborhood: haphazard
stacks of discarded wood,
crumbling sidewalks, piles of trash
sprawling by roads
children stepping slowly
through them, searching
for glass or old pans or copper wire,
while a gray cow stares dully
past the traffic, chewing and chewing
a blue plastic bag.

It's just that there's so much
of everything: so much color
in the markets, piles of yellow turmeric
and red vermilion, colors colliding
unexpectedly in salwar kameez
— bright yellow, bright red, hot pink —
and saris covered with mirrored sequins
and gold embroidery.
                                      So many people
walking on streets, not sidewalks,
skirting so many street dogs
playing or fighting or sleeping
on medians, inches from so much
traffic, so many men clutching
the open doors of a crowded buses,
or hanging halfway out
of overfilled auto rickshaws

or standing on street corners,
drinking chai, impassively watching
the women, who never pause, who walk
with purpose, always. So many eyes
and cell phone cameras trailing her
as she picks her way through
parks and national monuments.

Her exhaustion is finally justified.

So much pollution. It lodges in her
lungs, it clogs her pores, it clings
to the dry ends of her hair,
to the consternation of so many aunties
with so many opinions — she is breaking
out again, she should buy ayurvedic soap,
she should get married already, she has lost
too much weight. The aunties dish out judgments
like food, often along with it:
another syrupy gulab jamun, another dosa, another
spoonful of dal. The chilies tingle.
The sweetness is more than she can take.

She inhabits the superlative.

She learns to bargain like an Indian auntie
but usually just says *fuck it,* pays double,
and makes a crack about *white tax.*

She makes friends, so many friends,
bright flashes of laughter. They dissolve like mist
when she tries to pull them close.
She takes a lover, then another, weaving
her fingers between their fingers
until the city reclaims them.

She hadn't realized: between the fluttering
bus horns, the car horns, the flat motorcycle horns,
between the neighbor's harsh Hindi curses, the hiss
and screech of cats fighting, the dogs'
crepuscular cascade of howling, there is still
so much silence, more than enough
for a man to disappear.

She is the least overwhelming thing
in Delhi. There is just so much more
to long for, her throat dry
in the dry Delhi heat. She switches on
the ceiling fan and sprawls
alone on her bed. A mosquito hovers
just outside the hot air's swirl and rush,
waiting to see whether she will slide
one foot off the side of the bed,
whether the air around her will finally settle.

SAMSARA

In another life, says my Indian friend,
and it would explain so much,
never lost when I was lost
in Amsterdam, and of course
that tree in the Vondelpark, right there,
right by the river.

When haven't I wanted to believe?
My mother called me briefly away
from my sixth birthday party. I looked out
the upstairs window and saw my friends
still climbing the monkey bars,
still swinging, shouting to each other.
How I raced downstairs. How I forced my way
onto the swing set, as if
I had never left, as if I could insist
there be no world without me.

RAPTURE SCARE
"Falsehood is never in words; it is in things." Italo Calvino

The saucepan bubbled
over on the stove,
no one stirring;
the phone that called
my mother next door
beeped insistently,
off the hook.
In the next room,
the couch, dark
and angular under
the zig-zagged afghan,
the television's imperfect copy
of voices in the empty
house crowded with things
and me, certain
the thief in the night
had come and left me
with everything.

OUTLIERS

The Model A and Model T in their sheds
were permitted: I could clamber and scramble
around them, twist their steering wheels, pretend
I was Mister Toad stealing a motorcar. Not so
my grandfather's grandfather's tools, lying
in the fields behind the house: a rake, a cutter,
discs and drills, a rain-rough plough
sunk in and knotted to the ground
by prairie grasses, leaning into the wind.
Grandpa would not let me touch
the feral things. I had to hold them
only in my gaze, framed by the grass
and sky above our land. They had a chance
at a second life, setting the mood
as artworks at a western boutique hotel,
their rust rustic, smoothed
to an echo of neglect.
A man came with a checkbook.
But Grandpa preferred nothing
to not-enough, so they stayed
on our land until he lost it all,
braced by wind and held
from far away.

LOST SHEEP

What a picture
        (it was always a picture, a cartoon
cut-out patted onto the blue
        felt of a Sunday school easel, or
a dark and somber painting
        in a gilt frame): Christ
carrying the rescued lamb
        in the crook of his elbow
or pushing thorns aside, perhaps, the lamb
        draped around his neck.
Christ disheveled, a cut on his cheek
        representing everything
he suffered for this one
        lost sheep. I eyed
the sheep, with whom each artist
        willed me to identify
—willful, reckless, foolish, sought
        and held—and I could not.
God, it seemed, like everyone, loved
        a rebel, and I was not one
to toss my head and trot off
        just because. No,
I'd be outside that gilded frame,
        I and the ninety-nine,
and while the shepherd sought
        the runaway, I would stay
where I was left
        unguarded, too afraid to move.

LOOKING FOR PRESTER JOHN

The West longed for Prester John,
the way my friend Kiran longed to know the Roma,
sneaking backstage after their concert in Chicago.
They saw she was Indian, and the darkest man
broke away to greet her. With both of his hands,
he grabbed both of her hands, and his eyes
welled up when they met hers, and he said
…something in Romani she could not understand.

He paused, then started counting in Romani: *ek…do…teen…*
And she joined him in Hindi: *chaar…panch…cha…*
For it has only been a thousand years
since the Roma came out of India,
and though their tongues have shifted
into difference, they still share numbers.
Kiran and the man counted together,
chanting their last linguistic link,
until everyone burst out laughing,
Kiran still gripping the man's hands.

As for Prester John, there was hope,
for didn't Portuguese missionaries travel
all the way to India to find
Christians already there?
No, it didn't end well: squabbles
and splits over power, pride, the usual.
Mostly, we injure what we touch, casually
brushing dust off butterfly wings.

But who doesn't covet that dawning
recognition, like a stranger beside you telling

a version of a story you thought
your grandmother made up just for you?

Again, I find myself
in India. Again,
there are days I cannot bear
to leave my flat.
I leave it anyway.
Surely Prester John is here
somewhere, in some narrow,
angled lane, lowering a bucket
from a fourth floor balcony
to the chai wallah, or choosing
bitter gourds at the vegetable cart.

Surely he will smile, *There you are.*
Surely he will call for his family, our family,
and surely they will come
by ones and twos, so many,
too many to count, but we will try:
we will count together: *ek…do…teen…*

EARLY DINNER ENDING WITH A LINE FROM THOMAS MERTON

It begins like a joke: A woman walks into a bar
                 and bellies up to the bar,
                 and brays,
Ya got any of that lemon-cello?
                 I wanna try some, have ya heard of it?

I am reading at a table near the bar.
                 This is a Vietnamese restaurant,
      the bar secondary and, even on my first visit I can guess,
                 low on Italian liqueurs.
The Vietnamese bartender has heard of limoncello
                 and pours her a scotch.
                     I cringe
because she is loud and clueless
                 and has frizzy hair
   and the small man trailing behind her
                 does not remove his aviator sunglasses.
                       And she is wearing spandex pants
that stretch so much, as the old joke has it, because they *have* to.
                    And I snickered
   at that joke as a teenager and, by extension, at everyone
                 it made me think of,
    and wouldn't it serve me right someday,
to put on fifty pounds?
              Better to watch the waiter
and two waitresses at the other end of the bar,
       in quiet camaraderie,
               fold silverware into napkins
        before the dinner rush, while there's still time.

    Though the woman and the man have settled in now,
they are regulars here, maybe friends: the bartender knew
    her drink and has shed his proprietor's hustle
      and smiles and lingers where they sit,
drifting only occasionally
      to speak with his staff at the other end of the bar,
   where someone with an eye for whimsy has dropped
      a red cocktail umbrella into one long red straw
         in a glass of long red straws.

    The joke's on me, of course,
  because there's no need to cringe
for anyone, even for me, alone
     and reading by a bar, of all pretentious things,
because my plate is clean,
  and I don't want to stare, but I don't want to read, or go,
    because we are here, all of us
      together, which I had to sit alone to recognize,
tucking napkins around silverware, bringing food
     or eating, chatting, drinking scotch
    instead of limoncello,
       all walking around shining like the sun.

ROUAULT IN L.A.

Rouault, I have found you again, and just in time.
Who knew you could live
at LACMA? Such an easy museum:
light, open, airy. So California. So, let's face it,
not like your dark
crusted paintings, or like Paris,
where I first found you.
I was eighteen and did not know
all the things I still don't know
and then some, though I did know
a whole network of tunnels ran
through me, like the sewers under Paris,
that they threatened to overflow
at any moment, sometimes melancholic,
like the city's proud squalor, sometimes bleak
as that block of concrete high rises in the 15th.

Usually, my sorrow could find no form – until that painting
in a dim hallway at the Centre Georges Pompidou:
a rough, beige human figure,
featureless, on black. That was all.

I knew so little of art.
But I knew this artist knew
suffering, and wondered how, until
I saw the next room
filled with lumpy portraits of circus folk –
ungainly dancers, morose clowns –
and Christ after Christ – whippings, crucifixions,
tombs – which I did not love
as well as that first painting, not right after
the first shock of it, like lovers meeting.

Now I have lost my lover.
And you have returned to me:
your thick black lines, your mess,
your smudged shadows lurking
behind that California light, that ease, that energy
for as many takes as it takes.

Rouault, I confess
I have ignored you.
I wanted my heart
unbroken by the ordinary
departures that mark
and mark me. I wanted a deep breath
after a long cry. Forgive me for longing
for art to be merely pretty, as if I could stand
before your defiant circus girl,
your dark, sad clown, your dying Christ, and see
only your thick brushstrokes, your color in bold blocks,
and not the grief – mine, theirs – that holds me
here, that will not let me walk away, my breath
gratefully quickening.

FORGET ROME

If we must forget something, forget Rome.
Forget prosecco at midnight, a toast
to a writer we don't really know.
Forget wandering the streets at 3 a.m., seeking
that fifth bottle of wine that did us in,
barely catching the bar before closing.
Forget sleeping till one the next afternoon
and you grumbling at the day half gone.
Forget our Vatican visit, the Raphael loggia
I barely saw, so eager was I
to prove I knew my Bible, to identify
prophets, apostles, and parables.
Forget the Swiss guards saluting
in their loud Michelangelo outfits,
not, our friend quipped, his best work.
Forget the pastries leftover
from the Pope's name day, forget
the rosaries he blessed.

But that we landed in Denver late, so late,
two of our three flights delayed,
and that we drove, too tired to drive,
back to Wyoming, and finally arrived
at three a.m., beyond jet-lagged,
to find a goat -- a goat! -- tethered
in the neighbor's yard, mournfully bleating,
as we lugged our luggage inside,
that we told the story
over and over, and it was still funny
long after our bags were emptied and stowed
in the basement, where the dust bunnies

are fruitful and multiply, because
there could have been no clearer sign
that we were home? Remember that.

A LITANY IN TIME OF DIVORCE

I am the rushing in
                        my stopped   ears

I am the stone in my stomach
                              sinking
I am the glass half-empty
                          emptied
                by half

I am the first drunk day
                        dizzy
        the sun still up

I am the memories
                      that spring like traps

          as I walk through the house

I am the memories that crumble
                              like old bones
                                  lifted to light

WHY I SWITCHED THE MUSIC OFF

I wish the words came easy, like the sweet spill of time
through films set in some ideal past, the camera panning lazily
across English countryside, misty green against mistier green,
or following, in slow motion, a woman walking, her tiny,
    perfect ass
sewn into red silk. O'Keeffe called singing *the most perfect
form of expression.* She said, *because I cannot sing, I paint.*
I want to sing so beautifully that I am finally loved.
I want to stop a mugging with only the purity of my gaze.
I want actors to fight over who plays me in the quiet film,
that will get the star taken seriously as an artist.
I believe. As the old joke says of baptism, I seen it done.
I was in love with a man who swallows the world.
But he held me in his cheek like a stone he found in his food.
And look how I sleep: awake late, late into the quiet,
then half the day gone. The world is not enough with me
in my haze of fantasy or migraine, curtains drawn
against the glare and the heat of the day.
O singers, I can only listen to so many songs.

NIGHTMARES PLAGUE THE MESSY GIRL AS SHE TRAVELS

She thought she was going so far away, but everyone has followed. Her knuckle just caught a man on the side of the head as she rushed down the staircase. It's former U.S. President George Herbert Walker Bush. Sure, he says *that's okay* and smiles, but who else is watching? Her old boss Anne sneaks her into the better hotel. Now she can get those mini bagels she was so excited to share with everyone. A shiny cart, cloth napkins over little baskets. But whoops! she has eaten all but three. She didn't want to want them all to herself. Now the boy she yearns for is angry to see her. She's waiting in a sleepy room. Outside, rhythmic hammering. She sent two texts. She knew they'd make no difference. No matter how clever. No matter how many perfect words.

THE MESSY GIRL FORGETS HER DREAMS

over breakfast, luring wakefulness
with coffee, buttered bread.
But all day something hovers
just beyond sight: she starts
at a touch on the shoulder, a tap
at the door. On the bus ride home,
schoolgirls whisper
gravely to each other: *You dreamed
you were falling? You know,
if you hit the ground,
you won't wake up.*

THE SURVIVOR

The detective shut your front door behind him
and walked calmly toward us
across the lawn. He did not hurry
because he had no reason to hurry.

My second thought:
This is going to fuck me up for a long time.

There was no first thought.

Because you were alive
the last time I showered,
I put it off as long as I could.
I'm not stupid. I knew
it wouldn't stanch my grief.
I just wanted to carry the world
that had you in it
that much longer, if only
those few microns of cells
at the surface of my skin
and the slick of oil on my scalp
that touched the air we shared.

Though when I finally caved, I scrubbed
my skin red, I lathered my hair
twice, I deep conditioned
my sad split ends. I shaved.
Because this is what the living do:
we exfoliate. Then we stand
and we weep for our dead
till the water runs cold.

All I remember about your body
in its casket are the thick, black sutures
across the top of your bald head, and
the color of your skin: darkened,
mottled, like you were one big bruise.

Perhaps I should have taken
another look, a longer look,
but how long can anyone stand
before a miracle, and your body
stitched and purpled and emptied, was
a miracle: wine back into water,
water back into the rock.

A few books, a few candles, a few tools
in the garage. A few pans in the kitchen,
a few games by the TV. That's all.
In the bedroom, no pictures to take down, no clutter, just
your smartwatch charging neatly on its stand.
How little clothing there was to take to Goodwill:
four pairs of pants, twelve tee shirts, two suits.
How little of yourself
spilled into the things around you.
How lightly you walked on the earth.

I push my foot into my boot, and you die.
I put my toothbrush on its stand, and you die.
I put on my headset, and you die.
I fix myself tea, I order Thai food, I smudge
the surface of my tablet, and you die.
I find the plushie you gave me
for Valentine's Day, and you die a little harder.
You die as I walk past the gas station on 51st,
past Alex and Alix's apartment,
past the Chili's at 45th and Lamar.
I click the key into the ignition,
the radio switches on, and you die.
A pothole jars my right front wheel, and
you die, you die, you insist
on dying. You always were
a stubborn ass, but I can be stubborn, too.
I can hold out as long as it takes
for you to listen. Listen:
That's enough dying, now.
You can stop, now.
That's enough.

Last visit to your house, carrying out your drill, your hoodie, the last food in your fridge.

Last squeeze of the conditioner you said smelled like your grandma.

Last text from one of your friends saying I can call them anytime, they mean it, anytime.

Last conference call with your name still on the agenda, last email from you in my inbox, your last text falling off the bottom of my screen.

Last clean tee shirt you washed for me, whiff of dryer sheet over my face.

Last car wash coupon from the pack you bought me.

Last handful of the sriracha peas you left at my door.

The cashmere scarf I gave you for your birthday, the last thing in the world that smells like you.

My instructor says *dead body pose*
seventeen times during hot yoga,
which is, as they say in Hollywood,
a little on the nose, especially since
I'm lying on your yoga mat.
Even I find that kind of morbid, but
it's a really nice mat.
You only used it for a month
while we were breaking up, and
not even every day, at that.
It bothers me more that
when your yoga teacher said
set your intention at the start of class,
you directed your thoughts to me,
leaning into my leaving
instead of your own body.

I come because I am only body
here, in the heat.
You left me with so much
to not think about, and here
I can't think of anything,
can't think of you at all, until
I have nothing to do but
lie here. *Savasana,*
my teacher says, *Relax.*
Dead body pose. I think of you
thinking of me, my absence filling you
as your absence fills me now.
Relax, says my teacher, again,
and I try, I still my limbs,
I slow my breath, but there
you aren't. *Savasana,* he says again.
Dammit. *Dead body pose.*

The books name us "survivors."
That is what you made us
when, unmaking yourself, you
made yourself a thing
to survive.

Your absence is no more like hunger
Than any lack, except that
I feel it in my stomach.
Except that it intrudes,
it nags. It persists.

Except that sometimes
I miss you without noticing, then
notice, like realizing,
ravenous, that I've been
hungry for a while now.

No, your absence is not
particularly like hunger, though
I've also never been
hungry and also certain
I would never eat again.

I speed, late as usual,
to the preta karma
thirteen days after your death.
You hated my driving.
Slow is smooth,
you said, again and again,
smooth is fast, but
I never slowed down.

In your brother's living room,
your white friends sit solemnly,
trained by church, while
your Indian friends relax
and chat quietly, trusting
the ritual will go on
just fine without them.

Marigolds draping
your photo, spot of vermilion
on your forehead, the drone
of the pandit's chant: the atheist in you
would have hated all of it, but
you left. You don't get to pick.

The pandit says your journey
to the afterlife takes a day
for you, but a year for us, that finally
you were leaving, having lingered
these thirteen days. I haven't felt you
at the ceremony, though,
or at your house, or your memorial.
Even my dreams, when I dream of you,
are only dreams. Perhaps,
as usual, you left early.
Lord knows you hate to be late.

Couldn't you linger
just a little longer, just this once?
Slow is smooth,
smooth is fast. Surely
you can make up the time.

How like a car crash
it was: I, the unwitting
passenger, and you,
the locked door,
the steering wheel
that won't turn, the foot
on the gas pedal speeding
us inexorably toward
the impact
that flings me through
the windshield,
which is—unlucky
for both of us—also you.

Now shards of you
lodge in my flesh, and
after the road rash
scabs over, after
what looks like healing, you
work your way
to the surface, slicing me
open from inside.

Memory is no longer safe.
I brave it anyway.
I pull each piece of you
from my flesh and hold it
to the light, I turn it
and turn it—slick of blood, glint
of each jagged edge—before
I lay it aside, I bandage
each fresh wound, and I wait
for the next, for it seems
you are inexhaustible.

You are not inexhaustible
anymore. But I could gather
your family, your friends,
your lovers, we could pluck
all the shards from our flesh,
pass them around,
piece them together, and still
we would not have all of you,
though we do,
we gather and share, holding
memories bright with blood
up to the light, and
what's left of you glitters
like gems, or like sun on water, or
like glass by the side of the road.

The last time I saw you, you gave me a book of shitty poems. The second poem in one section, you said, particularly made you think of me. But three and a half hours of talk had wrung me out; I was desperate for rest; it didn't register which section that was.

The book is broken into four sections. Each section starts with a shitty proem of sorts, also in verse, which complicates things, as I cannot be sure whether you were counting those as poems or not. That narrows the field, then, to eight shitty poems. I'm fairly certain it is the second shitty poem in the first section, but that is merely an educated guess.

All I can know is that, when I hold this book, I hold a shitty poem that bound us without my participation or knowledge (one of a possible eight), and that I will never now have reason to lie about not hating it, that earnest, cringeworthy, shitty poem, whichever one it is.

First morning, first week, first thirteen days

First xanax I took to sleep.

First moment not thinking about you, then thinking about you.

First funny thing I thought, for an instant, that I would tell you later.

First meal at your favorite pizza place, first stop at the taco truck alone.

First drive north on 183 toward your house

First time I saw the fan in your bedroom unmoving.

First day I didn't cry.

First question I wished I'd asked you

First question I wished you were here to ask.

First night I slept without xanax, almost until dawn.

How are you holding up?
is the best way to ask, is the way
we ask each other the question
to which there is no good answer.

But surely there is a word
in another language, a phrase coined
by Kierkegaard or the Buddha,
meaning *today I am at my most*
human, meaning
I am not okay and
I'm okay

THE SHIFT

Today
    despite my usual preference
        for things I can't quite see
    (mist over mountains
reflections
    of the countryside in the opposite
        window of the train
    grand old houses
almost hidden
    by a thick cross-hatch
        of leaves) the glare
    of the sun on the lake
bothered me
    for once
        I wanted to see
    what was beyond it, I wanted
clarity
    instead of things suggesting
          something else.

PRAYER WITH MATHEMATICS
"This is not mathematics; this is theology."
  – Paul Albert Gordan

I met a philosophy professor who believes
   and also has a doctorate in mathematics,
a rare thing all around, though
   I nearly studied math.
I hated proofs but loved the thought
   that some infinite sets are greater than others.
If God speaks to man, wrote Poincaré,
   he uses the language of mathematics,
for what could you inhabit but
   theorems, esoteric
and pedantic as prayer, language
   of fixed points
and impossibility, inversion
   and reciprocity, embedding,
approximation, and convergence?
   I am still guilty of trying
to define you as what I have
   or have not touched,
despite the day I rode
   the bus from the South Side
downtown, alone
   and heartbroken; everyone
looking down, staring
   out the windows; a low dirge
droned and thrummed
   my sternum, and as we turned
from Balbo onto Michigan, another
   vibration, algorithmic
counterpoint to sorrow,
   one breath in

and out. It stopped.
    It was enough. It was you,
wasn't it, and years of sifting
    through corollaries, principles, postulates,
and all the handwaving and abstract nonsense
    reduce to one
brief intersection: jostling bus,
    anonymous neighbors, me,
and you, infinitesimal,
    infinite, bounded
by the limit of my need?

FARMER'S MARKET ELEGY

for Craig

Here are the fruits of summer mixed with fall:
the last of the Last Chance peaches, stacks of apples
arranged from tart to sweet. And, oh, the pears!
The Sekel pears are out! I look for you
because, if you came back, you would be here
near food and crowds. The way a cat won't leave
the door when someone's taking a shit inside,
or fucking inside, anything elemental.
You find the source. You will not be left out.
You're muttering to yourself now, aren't you,
and rolling your eyes when one loud man proclaims
"Non-toxic sprays" just means they kill you slower,
and dumps the peaches back out of his bag.
You're eying avocados greedily.
So plentiful, so varied here in Cali,
but what a pain they were to find in Rome.
And surely, dear, that's your unbodied hand
on a woman's freckled shoulder. She just wants
Honeycrisp, till you whisper, and she sees
another bin. *Oh, you have Macintosh?*
she asks me, *Those are tart, right? I'll take three.*
No, make that four. They shouldn't all be sweet.

ABOUT DAY EIGHT

Day Eight's vision is to be part of the healing of the world through the arts, and our mission is to empower individuals and communities to participate in the arts through the production, publication, and promotion of creative projects.

Day Eight's programming includes an online magazine, poetry events, live arts programming, book publishing, arts journalism, and education programs for children and youth.

Example 2021 projects include:

The DC Arts Writing Fellowship was created to support early career arts writers. The project is conducted in partnership with local news outlets including Tagg Magazine and The DC Line. An annual conference brings together leaders in the field of arts journalism.

The DC Poet Project is a poetry reading series and open-to-all poetry competition that supports the professional practice of poetry. The 2020 instance of the DC Poet Project was produced through support from the Wells Fargo Community Foundation and the National Endowment for the Arts.

Day Eight's projects in local art history included an online archive dedicated to DC's first artist cooperative gallery, the Jefferson Place Gallery.

All of Day Eight's projects are made possible by the support of volunteers and individual donors, including the Board of Directors. To learn more about the organization please visit www.DayEight.org.